Bubble

Kieran Hurley

methuen | drama

LONDON • NEW YORK • OXFORD • NEW DELHI • SYDNEY

METHUEN DRAMA
Bloomsbury Publishing Plc
50 Bedford Square, London, WC1B 3DP, UK
1385 Broadway, New York, NY 10018, USA
29 Earlsfort Terrace, Dublin 2, Ireland

BLOOMSBURY, METHUEN DRAMA and the Methuen
Drama logo are trademarks of Bloomsbury Publishing Plc

First published in Great Britain 2022

Series design by Rebecca Heselton

Cover image © morokey/shutterstock

A catalogue record for this book is available from the British Library.

A catalog record for this book is available from the Library of Congress.

ISBN: PB: 978-1-3503-9838-2
ePDF: 978-1-3503-9839-9
eBook: 978-1-3503-9840-5

Series: Modern Plays

Typeset by Mark Heslington Ltd, Scarborough, North Yorkshire

To find out more about our authors and books visit
www.bloomsbury.com and sign up for our newsletters.

Bubble

This play was originally developed as part of The Royal Conservatoire of Scotland's MA Classical and Contemporary Text Programme with support from the Playwrights' Studio, Scotland. It was later developed as a digital theatre production by Theatre Uncut, commissioned by The Space.

Characters

Anna Martinez, *undergraduate student*
Connor Whitelaw, *undergraduate student and soccer player*
Courtney Wheeler, *undergraduate student and student journalist*
Jane Jennings, *postgraduate student*
Hannah River, *undergraduate student and feminist activist*
Preston Cleeves-Nordek, *undergraduate student and a loner*
Ruth Holybank, *undergraduate student, first year*
Prof. William Barrett, *senior lecturer in History*
Dr Naomi Hoefferscheid, *lecturer in Sociology*
Coach John Hornsby, *soccer coach, and lecturer in Sports Science*

Scene

Digital space. In the online social media interactions between a group of students and staff of a well-regarded university. Now.

Writer's note

Bubble *was originally written as a commission for the Playwrights' Studio, Scotland, and the Royal Conservatoire of Scotland (RCS) to be performed by students on the RCS MA in Classical and Contemporary Text. It was developed in collaboration with director Shilpa T-Hyland and the cast Madison McLean, Charlie Clee, Dani Nelson, Kate Dylan, Courtney Keir, Ryan Wilson, Ivy Charles, Leo Graham, Megan Montgomery and Caitilin McCoy and owes a creative debt to their collective work.*

Stage it however you like. You should feel free to change or update references to the social media platform being used as you see fit. Have fun with it.

Loud noise. A short burst of static.

Courtney   omfg I totally can't believe he said that – that's hilarious

Ruth   It was kind of funny right?

Connor   pretty surprised to hear you guys say that tbh I mean it felt pretty out of line at the time

Anna   it really honestly wasn't that big of a deal like srsly everyone needs to chill the fuck out around here 📷 ▾

Connor   Ok, fair enough. You're cool with it then Anna? Just checking.

Hannah   wtaf is this bullshit? Is this shit for real?

Connor   Yeah like I said, happened today.

Hannah   Fuck this! Totally tagging some people into this shit, people have to see this.

Anna   I seriously don't give a shit about it but whatever 📷

Jane   Hey Hannah – you've tagged me into this but I can't see the OP. Maybe ask your friend or whoever to change the privacy settings thx

Hannah   hey Connor can you change the privacy settings so my friend can read this?

Connor   Sure. Done.

Hannah   You see this Jane?

Jane   Yes

Connor   So. Today in old Billy Barrett's history class something totally weird and inappropriate happened. It was the first class on the civil rights movement. I guess it's a popular subject because it was fuller than usual – so like, people were still all standing in the aisles and chatting and stuff when big Prof B.B. came in. And he was just standing there all flustered – you could see it had kind of thrown him the poor bastard. Eventually B.B. Gun starts asking everyone to settle down, doing a kind of high school teacher act but still trying to be all chummy and down with the kids you know? Everyone slowly shuts up, but some of the girls are still chatting and laughing and big old William Billiam sort of sheepishly joins in and laughs and is all like 'ladies, ladies, I'd quite like to start now if you please.' Anna – bit cheeky – says something like 'let's go then William, time's ticking on.' And old Billy B-bag – bless him – I dunno if he thinks she's flirting or whatever. He honestly goes and says:

'Well – ha ha – I would "crack on" thank you very much if I didn't have to be heard over a bunch of giggling sluts first!'

Jane   Well this is just obviously completely out of line.

Hannah   right?

Jane   He called her a *slut*? A senior professor? Saying that? To publically shame a teenage girl. I can't even.

Ruth   I'm not sure he was trying to shame her but it was pretty weird.

Connor   I agree it's not on.

Anna   hello-o! I honestly do not give a fuck?

Ruth   hey Courtney, is this like the kind of thing you could write about for the student paper?

Courtney   Honey, unless it's sports stories or funding scandals those boys aren't interested – trust me I've tried

Ruth   oh that sucks

Courtney   'Gotta be something that generates traffic babe.'

Preston   hey so I just wanted to say that I think professor william barrett is a pretty cool guy and like did you guys know that his wife left him a few years ago and actually he's super lonely and like maybe he was just excited and trying to make a joke or something? so like yeah I think people should slow down before you start jumping down someone's throat for what they can and can't say and maybe hold off making it open season on people who've just made a mistake and want to be liked

Connor Hi Preston. Do I know you? I don't think I'm friends with you on here.

Preston you're not my friend. none of you guys are friends with me. it's a public post I thought this was a free country

Hannah it's the settings, Connor anyone can post here now

Preston i know who you are though. everyone knows who you are. connor the sports guy. nice guy connor who all the girls like right?

Connor Um. Thanks?

Preston i posted more thoughts on this – but even those of you that know me on here probably didn't see it because your algorithms have all figured out to just skip over me so you can ignore me just like irl – algorithms are pretty cool like that huh?

Connor Look pal, I dunno what your beef is but nobody is making it 'open season' on anyone here ok, I like the guy too but that chat was awful.

Hannah Preston were you even there? you seem pretty keen to be an authority on this given you weren't even there?

Preston no I wasn't there I don't even take his class. i know him from the settlers of Catan society and I think he's a harmless guy

Ruth Settlers of Catan lol

Preston it's a rly good game stfu

Jane Ok. Preston. This isn't about whether Barrett is a 'good guy' or not.

This is about what behaviours are and aren't challenged in a university dominated by men in teaching positions.

Hannah   with an overwhelmingly white student population

Jane   Yes

Hannah   and very few people of colour in teaching positions, and a laughably poor LGBT inclusion policy, and next to no students from lower income families

Jane   Those are important but not necessarily relevant

Hannah   They're completely relevant

Preston   well I've just read the rest of this thread and it looks like the girl he said it to doesn't think it's a big deal either so hahaha f u

Anna   it's true I completely don't

Preston   SEE??!!!!11!!1!

Hannah   oh so you're gonna mansplain sexism to us now huh Preston?

Preston   FFS!!

Jane   Ok this conversation got ridiculous very quickly, I'm out. Preston I'm blocking you. Nothing personal I've just had way too much crap on here lately and can't deal with this bullshit in my tl rn

Preston   blocking me! you're fucking hilarious you people, you know that? it's like randy p says, you're like fucking nazis or something

Anna   lol who the hell is Randy P?

Preston   oh you don't know Randy P? you're gonna *know* randy p believe me

Hannah   let me guess you're gonna tell us how being blocked by Jane is a violation of your **free speech** now right? 🙄

Preston   what if I am

Hannah   write this down: free speech ain't the same thing as other people having to listen to your BS

Preston   fucking NAZI!

Anna   hey, I'm not taking sides with this weirdo btw – I definitely don't know this guy for the record I don't wan't anybody thinking I'm friends with this cheeseball. I'm just saying I literally give zero fucks about any of this

Ruth   did he really call you a slut? I just read somewhere else he said hussy. that seems less bad. is that less bad?

Anna   I. Don't. Care.

Hannah   it's every bit as bad FFS

Courtney   Hussy? For real? Like dude what are you somebody's creepy uncle?

Anna   right? like what are you some divorced detective in a TV cop drama?

Courtney   Like what are you some kind of British military officer pervert away from home, missing his housemaid?

Anna   LOL. hey BB!! the 1970s called – they want their workplace banter back!

Ruth   yeah like what are you some kind of pervert!

Courtney   Ruth I feel we kinda already covered that sweetie

Connor   Hey I'm getting lots of share notifications on this from people I don't know.

Jane   Yeah. I shared this to the Feminist Society page, to move the conversation somewhere productive. I hope you don't mind.

Connor   Ok. Fine I guess.

Hannah   Connor do you have literally no idea how Facebook works or what?

What are you like 40?

Connor   Come on, who even uses Facebook? I use this thing for course stuff.

Jane   Thanks. It's generated quite a lot of interest

Connor   I see that.

Courtney   Hey Connor I see your post has really taken off. I'm actually thinking about writing a short piece on all this for the student paper after all. It's given me an idea. Have PMed you

Jane   It's started a really important discussion around representation on campus.

Connor   Ok. Well, good then.

Courtney   Hi Jane. I'm Courtney. I write for the student paper. Are you a member of the feminist society, can you PM me?

Ruth   Cool – go Courtney!

Anna   this is so stupid

Ruth   this is so funny!

Courtney   Hey Anna, hey Ruth – have PMed you

Loud noise. A short burst of static.

Hornsby   Hi there Connor. Coach Hornsby here. I notice your Facebook story here about my colleague has gained quite a bit of traction there son. Just want to add my voice to the clamour here to say that William Barrett is a decent kind of a man. I wonder if we could have a little chinwag about all this next time you're in for soccer practice, nothing heavy just a few words I'd like to say about my friend Professor Barrett here ok. Sound cool?

Connor   Sure thing John. Side note: You know you don't need to introduce yourself by name on this right, it shows up right there next to your profile pic 😊

Hornsby   Well seems I do need to introduce myself if you're gonna call me 'Janet' like that sonny! Told you once, told you twice, I'll tell you many times again – it's Coach! You hear? 😊

Jane   What is you want to say about Barrett, Coach?

Hornsby   With the greatest of respect to you Miss Jane, I'm not looking for a public debate here I was just reaching out to my friend for a conversation.

Hannah   'Miss Jane?' wtf?

Anna   Hannah, he's just old school. it's cool.

Preston   Yeah ha ha shut up FEMINAZI!!

Hornsby   Preston, son, you know your mother has asked me to monitor your online behaviour please treat the lady with respect.

Ruth   your **mom** Preston!!?! LOL

Hannah   OMG this is *gold* I'm crying

Anna   I'm dead. I'm literally dead right now. too good! 😂 😂 😂

Courtney   Hi Coach Hornsby, my name is Courtney I'm a reporter for the Student Gazette – could I PM you some quick questions about all this?

Hornsby   I meant no offence by that comment, it was not intended as a joke or as an insult to young Preston in any way, shape or form.

Anna   dying. dying. dead. 🔪

Preston   i hate you all

Loud noise. A short burst of static.

Barrett   Hi. John. I know you use this thing a lot, I hope you don't mind me contacting you here. You'll have seen I made a bit of a silly boo-boo and it seems to have kicked up quite a fuss. Anyway. I knew there was a lot of stuff being said about me on this thing so I started this account to have a look and – well gosh it's quite something isn't it? I wondered – you know you're an old friend – and I wondered if you had any advice on what I should do? I hope I'm not over-reacting but it does feel a bit like the dogs are circling and . . . Well. It has been a tough couple of years as you know. The job gives me focus. It's really all I have left. I'd quite like to just keep my head down and everything of course, but do you think if I made some kind or statement or apology or something that would help make all this just go away? Or would I just be fanning the flames?

I can't remember what I said you know. It just came out. And even if I did say it, did you know that etymologically speaking, the word 'slut' really only means an 'a woman who is untidy' – there was quite a lot of mess when I walked in. It wasn't exactly factually inaccurate.

Anyway.

I do desperately wish the students would all just shut up and settle down. Which, ironically, was kind of my point in the first place!

Sorry to contact you at this ungodly hour, but you know. It's on my mind a bit! Thanks for your time, old friend.

Yours, William.

Hoefferscheid   William. Hello. This is Dr Naomi Hoefferscheid here I think you've tried to send John a private message here a few hours ago but what you've actually done is post on his 'wall' – which means anyone can see it, and comment on it. Like I am, now. It's unlikely any of the students will have seen it because you're not connected to them on here. But John is, so they might. And I don't think you really want them to! Only you or John can delete this post so I'm just hoping you pick up this message.

Pause.

Hoefferscheid   Ok, you've not replied so I'm guessing you're not up yet. I'm gonna call you to make sure you see this ok?

Pause.

Hoefferscheid   You. Need. To. Delete. This. William.

Pause.

Barrett   Ooops! Naomi. Sorry. New to all this. How do I delete it?

Hoefferscheid   There's a little icon in the top right corner like a downwards arrow, click on it and a menu will appear, you see it?

Barrett   I can't see it.

Hornsby   Hey guys – yeah Bill, Naomi is right you really don't want to make this public buddy.

Hoefferscheid   John can you just delete it please?

Jane   Holy. Shit.

Hoefferscheid   Oh great. Hi Jane.

Jane   Is this for real?

Hoefferscheid   Jane, this is a complex situation that doesn't need to be inflamed any further, can we please talk about this?

Barrett   Oh dear. I did another booby didn't I? Did I do a booby?

Hornsby   Bill just stop writing things for a moment would you?! Jesus man.

Loud noise. A short burst of static.

Hannah   hi everyone so I'm totally reposting this screenshot that Jane took of William Barrett thinking that he's leaving a private message to Hornsby on here, and basically defending the word 'slut', referring to angry female students as 'dogs' and contemplating making an insincere political apology just to 'make it all go away' which I'm sure you'll agree is total BS

Connor   Oh. Oh dear.

Hoefferscheid   Jane. Have PMed you.

Jane   Naomi. Hi

Hoefferscheid   What in the hell Jane? The public conversation around this is getting out of hand. What are you doing, I thought we were friends?

Jane   Hannah posted it not me. I can't believe you're defending him, I respected you

Hoefferscheid   I'm not defending him, you know I think you're an exceptional student, I'm asking you to be mature about this.

Jane   Please don't patronise me, Naomi

Ruth   I do feel kind of sorry for Barrett he sounds kind of sad.

Jane   I really wish you'd spoken to me about this before going public with it Hannah

Hannah   why? you don't think people should know that this is his attitude to young women? hey Courtney – you seen this? wanna use it in your piece?

Courtney   Hi. Thank you. Yes. Definitely.

Loud noise. A short burst of static.

Preston   dear internet. so i guess this is just another random late night cry-for-help post about how nobody notices that i exist and i'm a failure in everything i do. i don't think i'm a bad guy i guess i must just be ugly. either way people hate me. what do you do to make women not ignore you? i'm a good person, i would be a good husband to someone one day but i'm not even in the friendzone, i'm in the nobody zone

i don't think people actually understand how that feels. like how it really feels

randy p says in his latest video that to be a white man in this society has become the worst thing you can be, the most demonised of all. maybe that's right I definitely feel hated. william barrett is pretty hated.

i guess this is just attention-seeking like i don't even know why i'm posting it, i must be such a loser. i wish i was strong. i wanna be strong like the way men are supposed to be like a warrior. i know i deserve better than this. i want to be able to take what i deserve. i wish i could. see i can write this here because i basically know nobody will read it which is the kind of hilarious irony. i guess i'll still delete it in a few minutes lol fml what a pathetic loser

Loud noise. A short burst of static.

Courtney   Ok, so setting this next post to restricted view basically so only some of you can see it. As you may know, I've been having a pretty hard time at the paper with basically all my suggestions and ideas being over-ruled by the bullshit boys' club that runs the thing. I know, great rehearsal for a career in journalism but seriously – this piece about slutgate I'm hoping can generate quite a lot of clicks. I know I'm a way better writer than any of the journo-bros on this two-bit magazine. If you all could give my article a boost by linking to it on your own pages and sharing it on other platforms I'd super appreciate it. Here's the link:

UNIVERSITY MANAGEMENT RELEASE STATEMENT ON SLUTGATE AND YOU JUST WON'T BELIEVE WHAT IT SAYS.

Loud noise. A short burst of static.

Ruth   hi – reposting this into the feminist society page so my new friends here can tell me what to think about this

Jane   You shouldn't let anyone tell you what to think Ruth.

Ruth   I know but you know. you know?

Hoefferscheid   The statement says: 'The University recognises the inappropriate nature of the language allegedly used by a member of staff towards an undergraduate student. Professor William Barrett is a valued member of our research community and he offers an unreserved apology for any offence caused. The University believes that in this age of social media, staff and students alike have a responsibility to discuss events with maturity. The matter is being handled internally and there will be no further comment.'

Hannah   so wait, it's not his fault for being a sexist asshole it's our fault for fucking *talking* about it?

Hoefferscheid   Well, let's hope this is the end of it.

Ruth   isn't it weird that we call scandals something-gate? slutgate. like it's after watergate right? but watergate wasn't a scandal about water – it was the scandal about watergate. so really when we talk about that it should be watergategate? right? or we should drop the 'gate' thing and just say scandal. SLUTSCANDAL. that works right?

Courtney   Sounds like an extremely lame punk rock band.

Anna   I would quite like everyone to shut up about this now please, it's getting embarrassing

Hannah   this isn't just about what Barrett said to you Anna. this is about wagon-circling a powerful man so he can get away with whatever, while telling women to shut up and stop being hysterical. it's victim-blaming logic, it's fucking endemic.

Jane   I think she's right Anna.

Anna   Well fine screw you guys. Everyone else send me cat pics. 🐱🐱🐱🐱🐱

Ruth   Here's one Anna look he's skateboarding! Squeee! So cute! Xxx

Anna   ◌ ◌ 🐱🐱🐱

Preston   hey look I figured you guys might be interested in this. WILLIAM BARRETT RESIGNS AMIDST SEXISM SCANDAL. click the link!

Anna   Holy shit Preston.

Jane   I can't see it I'm blocking him.

Hannah   I'll copy paste for you

'Never Gonna Give You Up' by Rick Astley plays.

Hannah   fuck you Preston

Preston   ha ha ha ha lolololol!!!!11!!! RRRICKROOOOLLLLLLED!!111!!!

Anna   What the hell is this? 😮

Hannah   rickrolling. It's so like 2013

Anna   have to hand it to him that's pretty funny

Jane   I don't get it. He's so weird.

Hannah   it's pathetic

Ruth   I love that song!

Preston   i hate you all

Loud noise. A short burst of static.

Jane   Following the events of what is now widely referred to as 'slutgate' the Feminist Society are calling an open meeting for women to share their experiences of campus sexism, and to discuss misogyny within the university at large. This isn't a campaign event or a protest. This is a space to build relationships and support. You don't need to be a member, or even call yourself a feminist – if you identify as a woman or non-binary and you want to meet others to talk about this then you are warmly welcome. We'll provide tea and coffee, you just bring yourself.

Please note, while this event is open to both undergraduate and postgraduate students of any level, at this moment due to a general air of mistrust in the University management we are not inviting staff to attend. Thank you for respecting this.

Hannah   cool nice work Jane

Jane   Thanks. It's a start at least.

Anna   L – O – motherfucking – L

Jane   Anna it'd be really great if you wanted to come though I appreciate you may not want to.

Anna   you're running with something that happened to *me* at the top of this, you know that right?

Hannah   she doesn't use any names

Anna   yeah well I want you to delete that bit, I don't want anything to do with this 😠

Jane   Sure we can do that, of course. Sorry for any distress Anna.

Ruth   I'm coming. it's exciting! is this like a protest? I've never been to a protest before?

Jane   That's great you're coming Ruth :) No it's not a protest, it's just a meet-up.

Anna   😾😾😾😾😾😾

Ruth   are you really pissed Anna?

Anna   🖕

Ruth   oh

Connor   I'll come. Sounds great.

Hannah   Um. No you won't.

Connor   What?

Loud noise. A short burst of static.

Hoefferscheid   Ok so here's something that might get me in a bit of trouble and I'll probably live to regret but to hell with it, I figure it's time some of us started being a bit more open about this.

I have been a class lecturer for nearly ten years. I consider myself socially and politically liberal, have always been active in progressive politics. I was an energetic campaigner for things like equal rights in my youth. And something has shifted in campus culture since I started out in this job. And I have to say: my students sometimes terrify me. The 'woke' ones most of all.

I used to include materials in my class that were intended to be difficult, to provoke, to be divisive and cause debate. Growing up as a young feminist we didn't cushion ourselves in bubble-wrap, we learned to develop thick skins to that which challenged and even hurt us. There is a growing trend now as I see it, for students not just to want to avoid challenging ideas, but to actually cry foul at any content in class that might be seen to hurt their delicate feelings.

Now I'm not for a second going to suggest that calling a young woman a 'slut' represents some uncomfortable nugget of critical thought. And God knows I've had my disagreements with my colleague Professor Barrett. But the response to this – it must be said – relatively minor transgression maps quite easily on to a more general and worrying trend which places teaching staff are at the mercy of a culture of witch-hunting from a supposedly socially liberal student body. A student body that is more concerned with using 'safe spaces' and 'trigger warnings' to protect individuals from perceived 'hurt' from words and ideas than it is with actually changing anything. I don't want to sound like one of these people crusading against 'identity politics' – look I'm a feminist ok – but the truth remains that 'feelings' are not where the root cause of injustice lies. And this preoccupation with defending feelings is not only a distraction from actually challenging injustice, it is increasingly clear that it is now actively dangerous in its own right.

Words aren't things. They're not violent. They're the carriers of ideas.

And frankly, this culture has become a threat to our jobs, our livelihoods, and our academic integrity.

Loud noise. A short burst of static.

Jane   It's a women's space Connor, but thank you for the interest. Maybe you could share the event?

Connor   wtaf? Wtf is this then?

Jane   It's just a meet-up.

Connor   That men are banned from?

Hannah   correct

Jane   Not 'banned' – it's just a space for women, that's all.

Connor   Can I just reasonably ask why?

Hannah   oh here it fucking comes . . .

Connor   I'm sorry, here what comes? I've been nothing but civil. It was after all, the fact that lots of people read my Facebook post that drew attention to this in the first place.

Hannah   oh well girls if we aren't just blessed to have him: it's Captain Save-A- Slut!

Connor   I find that language offensive and was under the impression that you did too.

Hannah   me using it is toootally different, brosef

Connor   How?

Ruth   I think he has a point maybe men should be allowed to come

Connor   Exactly, Ruth. Thank you.

Jane   Look. Connor. Thank you for raising attention to what was said in class that day. It helped kick start a discussion. But it's a discussion that's been needed for a long time. And the fact is that a lot of women are much less comfortable sharing experiences of sexism in the company of men. If you want to be an ally I'm sure there will be other ways you can be of help in the future too if you want to. Perhaps you could help by promoting this event? 😌

Connor   But I know lots of men that would want to come and listen and help.

Hannah   *sigh* then you can start by listening now, asshole

Connor   You're being rude. I've been nothing but polite.

Hannah   you started this thread by saying 'what the actual fuck is this' but whatever

Connor   I apologise. I will edit that. But why would you refuse my help?

Hannah   you really think the thing the feminist society is missing is the insight and abilities of men? is that actually your hot take on this?

Connor   You're distorting now.

Hannah   look: having men around makes a space unsafe for victims of sexism to talk about their experience – what is confusing you about this?

Connor   Is that what this is, one of those 'safe spaces'? Ruth you're not really going to go along and support this thing are you?

Ruth   I don't know

Connor   Christ. Look. That some women might find it hard to talk about this stuff around men is a point I hadn't considered. Now by engaging, I have my understanding improved. Do you see how that works? Yes? I still disagree but I have a fuller understanding. Debate changes things by changing minds. That's what free speech is all about.

Hannah   ok. bro? I'm not going to waste energy explaining this shit more than once. the thing is – as this conversation *aptly fucking demonstrates* – a lot of the time even *really well-meaning* men have a tendency to take up space and energy by focusing on themselves and on their experience, failing to *actually* listen, undermining women and demanding that time be spent on educating them in very. basic. shit. like. this. you're offended by safe spaces? the whole goddamn *world* is your safe space. we're just taking one tiny little time-out where we don't have to worry about what you might be thinking and tailor every single thing we say and do towards you and your point of view. this isn't *hiding* from debate. it's about actually having the difficult hard discussions that you – like it or not – simply get in the way of

Connor   I'm only trying to help.

Hannah   well I hate to break it you petal – but sometimes having you around is way more of a hindrance than a help, ok, no matter how much a Top Nice Guy you imagine yourself to be. because tbh, if you want to know what I think – I think that this conversation has way more to do with your own sense of entitlement than it does with actually helping women. so with the best will in the world sweetie, if you really genuinely want to prove me wrong maybe consider the possibility that there are other ways of helping which might be better than showing up in women's spaces wearing a t-shirt that says 'Look At What A Swell Dude I Am' and demanding that you be heard

Jane   Hannah, go easy on him.

Hannah   don't tone-police me Jane, I'm truly sick of this shit Connor: You've made your feelings perfectly clear. I'm out.

Ruth   well this has gone really well so far I think

Connor   Courtney – you wanted to talk to me for your article? I think I have a story for you.

Courtney   Awesome. PM me?

Connor   Sure.

Loud noise. A short burst of static.

Courtney   Hey, everyone, please like and share my new story: FEMINIST SOCIETY 'SAFE SPACE' MEETING MET WITH COUNTER-PROTEST FROM FREE SPEECH ACTIVISTS

Hoefferscheid   This is really excellent from one of my students on mollycoddled millennial campus culture. Please do read and share:

Courtney   Following the announcement of a women-only event to discuss sexism on campus, a group of free speech activists have staged a counter-rally in opposition to what they see as a culture of fear, inhibition, and censorship. Connor Whitelaw, a politics student who describes himself as feminist, organised the event. He had this to say:

Connor   As John Stewart Mill said: 'If any opinion is compelled to silence, that opinion may, for aught we can certainly know, be true. To deny this is to assume our own infallibility.' The people who have organised this event are choosing to live in a bubble, assuming themselves infallible and excluding a great number of men from their thinking and from helping with their cause. I think that's a terrible failing, but also a terrible crime against free speech and we're here to say that these 'safe spaces' ought to be abolished in favour of rigorous, open debate. This is a university. If you can't handle the heat, get out of the kitchen.

Hannah   free speech! free speech! freeze peach! I don't think you understand what freedom of speech *is* honeysuckle. it's not the same thing as being able to walk into any room and demand that people listen to you.

Hoefferscheid   John, Connor is one of your students right? I think he's taken an excellent and very important stand here.

Hornsby   I can't claim to understand entirely what's going on any more but I agree he is a good kid.

Barrett   Naomi. Hi. This is a private message I'm sending right?

Naomi   Right.

Barrett   Oh phew. They're not still talking about slutgate are they? Has it gone away yet?

Naomi   It doesn't look like it's going away for a while William.

Barrett   Oh bloody hell.

Courtney   The turnout of the event was far greater than anticipated, gaining traction with pro-free speech movements and, some have speculated with anti-feminist activists and men's rights activists – known as MRAs.

Connor   Thanks for the coverage Courtney – it really helped.

Preston   connor bro you totally owe me one

Connor   Why would that be?

Preston   i posted your event to a sub-reddit i post on. randy p says the alt-right is a free speech movement so i thought this was a great opportunity to make our mark on campus

Connor   Well. Anyone is welcome. We were glad of the numbers. So thanks I guess.

Preston   no thank *you* – man it was cool. guys like us, we're about pushing back against the restrictions placed on our freedoms by the libtards and feminist thought police who want to control what we can and can't say. and so like this was like a totally huge victory

Ruth   so I feel like I'm still catching up but wasn't Hannah's whole point the idea that men take up lots of space and time and energy and make it all about themselves?

Jane   Yup.

Ruth   lol

Anna   This is all such bullshit. If anyone needs me: insta. Or, I dunno email or whatever.

Hannah   jesus fucking christ will someone just literally fucking kill all men already

Courtney   Literally?

Hannah   yes fucking LITERALLY

Courtney   So you're not joking?

Anna   wait up Courtney, what are you getting at?

Loud noise. A short burst of static.

Courtney   Hey troops please like and share my new piece: FEMINIST SOCIETY SPOKESPERSON EMBROILED IN 'KILL ALL MEN' FACEBOOK POST CONTROVERSY

Hannah   oh ffs are you fucking kidding me?

Hoefferscheid   Well, this is interesting.

Barrett   Hey John. Just sending you a message here, in the private message box, for you to pick up when you see it.

Hornsby   Yes Bill. I think you have the hang of it now.

Barrett   Phew. Ok. So. This is good right? What she's said is worse than what I said, so that's good right?

Hornsby   I think this is getting fairly out of hand Bill, I have to say.

Barrett   You think this is going to put more scrutiny on me, or less? You know they've told me I'm 'under review' whatever that means.

Hornsby   Bill, I think this is going to put a lot of unhealthy attention on this young lady.

Barrett   Right. Well yes. She said a very, very unacceptable thing.

Hornsby   No. I think we need to do something about this.

Barrett   What do you mean?

Ruth   I don't think she really meant it like that did she?

Connor   It's kind of ironic, you have to admit that.

Ruth   ironic like how? i'm confused.

Hannah   oh great. here come the trolls. my inbox is bursting at the seams with fucking MRA bullshit. I can't log on here without wading through this shit

Jane   Everyone commenting on or sharing this story about Hannah, or jumping to conclusions about her, or saying things about her on here: please calm down. It's actually a fairly recognisable in-joke and quite obviously not a sentiment to be taken seriously.

Connor   How can you be defending her? Hypocrite!

Hannah   oh god. I can't do this. I can't do this anymore. you people are fucking sick

Hannah *disappears.*

Jane   Connor, I'm blocking you now.

Preston   TYPICAL FEMINAZI BS

Ruth   hypocrite how?

Connor Hannah can say what she wants about killing men but after slutgate she can hardly defend it as a misunderstood joke can she?

Jane It's totally, totally different.

Connor How?

Barrett God damn it John, they're still talking about slutgate.

Ruth hey Jane I just tried to message Hannah but I can't find her account?

Courtney Thanks for all the shares everyone, my story has been picked up and re-published on professional news sites, check it out I get paid and everything.

Ruth Jane?

Hoefferscheid Congratulations Courtney, great to see hard work rewarded.

Preston i think this is putting our school on the map you know. this is awesome, totally reposting

Courtney Please do share it widely, keep those clicks coming.

Ruth Hey Anna you're in this, look!

Courtney The whole incident has prompted student Anna Martinez, who herself was the subject of the original 'slutgate' incident, to finally break her silence on the issue of campus free speech. Anna spoke to us yesterday and had this to say:

Anna I don't give a shit about Hannah's joke. I don't give a shit about Barrett's joke. I think you're all fucking idiots. Leave. Me. Alone.

Courtney Hi Jane. Do you know how I can get hold of Hannah at all? Help a sister out?

Jane   Courtney. I notice you're getting a lot more articles published these days. I guess you must be generating a lot of web traffic huh.

Courtney   Yeah. I imagine I have you and your society's full support as a young woman attempting to succeed in a male-dominated area of university life, of course.

Jane   Go to hell. I hope you're proud of yourself.

Courtney   You know what? I sure am. Hey, I've not seen Hannah for a while. Has she deleted her account or what?

Jane   She's keeping a low profile thanks to you. You know she's been getting death threats on here right? You know that?

Courtney   What like real ones?

Jane   What does that even mean?

Courtney   Look it's just the ugly by-product of a high profile news story. It happens. It's nothing to be too alarmed about – I thought you were used to online abuse.

Jane   Death threats and rape threats, Courtney.

Courtney   You don't think they're real do you?

Jane   Oh I dunno you want me to ask her to send them over to you and you can read them verbatim?

Courtney   Ooh could you?

Jane   Go. Away.

Anna   Courtney will you seriously fuck off with this?

Courtney   Ooh, no emoji Anna I guess that means you're *being serious*

Anna   suck this 🔪

Courtney   Jane, do you know how I can contact her if she's not on here? I've got national level interest in this thing, it's a pretty big deal – can I speak to her?

Jane   Ok do you think I am just totally retarded or what?

Courtney   Careful I might run a story on your ableist language

Jane   I'm blocking you now fuck you.

Loud noise. A short burst of static.

Preston   bitches. listen up because it's our turn now:

Following recent high-profile controversies around free speech and censorship on campus, involving coverage on national news we are pleased to announce that RANDY P has responded by adding a late addition to his speaking tour: and he's coming here.

Men's rights activist and free speech vanguardist RANDY P is a leading figure of the alt-right – the new movement of young western conservatives opposed to political correctness and the culture of censorship.

Cometh the hour, cometh the man. Fresh from a lucrative new book deal and a rising profile, this event is sure to ruffle the feathers of the precious safe space liberal snowflakes and feminists who want to control what we can and can't say. Conservatism is the new rock and roll, populism is the new punk rock, and RANDY P is here to say unsayable truths so you better shut up and listen.

Anna   did you organise this Preston?

Preston   i might have helped get the ball rolling a little

Anna   who the hell is this guy? like Randy P? what are you a retired pro-wrestler sex addict?

Jane   Oh Jesus.

Ruth   what are you an erotica novel about a struggling RnB singer?

Anna   good one Ruth! 😨

Jane   This isn't funny. This guy is a monster. Check out his shit here, here, and here.

Ruth   Oh. Oh God.

Preston   deal with it bitches

Jane   We need to do something about this.

Loud noise. A short burst of static.

Courtney   Me again! Please share my longread feature: WHO IS RANDY P? A PROFILE OF THIS DAPPER AND SURPRISINGLY CHARISMATIC WHITE NATIONALIST

Anna   'charismatic white nationalist' – that means like 'charming and loveable nazi' right? lol

Courtney   Read the piece please, that's not what it says.

Ruth   Why are you giving air time to this guy Courtney?

Courtney   Why not?

Hoefferscheid   While it pains me to say it 'Randy P' has a right to be heard – but more than that silencing him just lends him power and legitimacy and plays into his hands.

Connor   Correct. However abhorrent his views the only way to defeat them is in the marketplace of ideas.

Jane   Bullshit.

Please share this.

The Feminist Society, in conjunction with University Diversity release the following statement:

We condemn in no uncertain terms the recent decision from University management to allow the controversial alt-right figure and misogynist white nationalist 'Randy P' to speak on campus. Randy P is a proponent of hate speech. We refuse to let our university become a place where the following views are legitimised under the guise of 'debate':

'Men and women are not equal. They were not made equal, born equal, nor should they try to be equal – it is an unnatural aberration.'

'The question isn't how best to integrate. The question is what races best serve the interests of our species as whole. Once we see that the black and Jewish races are a hindrance to our people's goals, the question becomes simply: what is the most expedient strategy for removing them.'

'It is a gross injustice that a man may be punished for so-called raping his own wife. She's his wife! She's his. Through all civilisations, history knows this.'

'Women and men are both happier when men can take action and behave like true warriors. When a woman says no: ignore her. It's what she wants you to do.'

Please signs our open letter opposing the decision to let this man speak. No platform for rape apologists. No platform for fascism.

Pause.

Connor No.

Ruth What?

Connor I can't. I can't sign it.

Ruth What the hell is wrong with you?

Connor Obviously I don't agree with him! Obviously! But you don't defeat these idiots by telling them they can't be heard!

Jane Connor, there are red lines asshole. If you believe in democracy, you don't make space for fascism. For fuck's sake!

Preston LOL typical SJW keyboard warrior bullshit!

Connor Jane. I thought you were blocking me. And Preston.

Jane   I've decided to keep an eye on you both.

Courtney   Hey everyone please like and share my new story: UNIVERSITY MANAGEMENT UNDER INCREASING PRESSURE TO TAKE A POSITION ON CONTROVERSIAL 'RANDY P' SPEAKING TOUR

Connor   Can't you see he's just going to use this to his advantage, to drum up support?

Jane   His 'advantage' is having people like you roll over and legitimise his ideas rather than to stand up to him. And even if he fucking is so what, we'll meet him on the streets.

Connor   Mob rule. You're as bad as the Nazis. Ruth, which side are you on here? You're supporting mob rule.

Jane   Newsflash Connor: protesting on the streets does not make you a Nazi.

Being an actual fucking Nazi makes you a fucking Nazi. Here's you: 'I'm so proud of my grandpappy's generation who fought the Nazis to defend our freedoms.' Also you: 'hey guys let's listen to this Nazi his opinions are valid.'

Preston   hate to burst your bubble bitches but it's a free country. connor don't listen to them bro. you know randy p has just announced he might pull out now out of safety fears for his fans and followers? who're the real nazis now huh?

Jane   That's a stunt. That's such an obvious PR stunt.

Anna   hey Preston, see this story I found: RANDY P WITH IMPORTANT MESSAGE TO STUDENT FOLLOWERS IN THIS DIFFICULT TIME – CLICK HERE

'Never Gonna Give You Up' by Rick Astley plays.

Preston   FUCK YOU

Anna   hahahhahahahaha suck my rickroll BITCH

👄 🏃 🎤 🎵 💃 🎵 😂 😂 😂 😂 😂 😂

Ruth   I love that song!

Hoefferscheid   Hello everyone. I wasn't meaning to post on here for a while until the atmosphere on campus cooled a little but in case you didn't know we're on national news: UNIVERSITY MANAGEMENT UNDER INCREASING PRESSURE TO TAKE A POSITION ON CONTROVERSIAL 'RANDY P' SPEAKING TOUR

Hornsby   I'm not sure about this. I'm really not sure about this.

Courtney   That's my story. What the fuck? They stole my story.

Barrett   Naomi. Have PMed you.

Hoefferscheid   Yes, William.

Barrett   The national news. It hasn't mentioned me. Or slutgate. Do you think it's moved on?

Hoefferscheid   I imagine it's probably not the focus of the story, William no.

Barrett   No. Right. No. Ok. Great. 👍

Hoefferscheid   You're talking in emoji now William?

Barrett   👌 😎 😌

Hoefferscheid   Jesus. We really are through the looking glass.

Barrett   🧍

Hoefferscheid   Stop it William.

Barrett   🔴

Hoefferscheid   William, what is happening out there is actually incredibly serious.

Barrett   😵 😵 😵

Courtney   'In this climate, where the University's commitment to open debate and free speech is being openly questioned – its next move will prove crucial and may be an acid for the political mood of the country.'

Assholes! Those are exactly my words. Does anyone know who I write to about this? Anyone? Hello?

Loud noise. A short burst of static.

Hoefferscheid   A STATEMENT FROM THE UNIVERSITY MANAGEMENT. I have to say I think all of us staff need to rally behind this position this point, however uncomfortable some people may be with it. So please share this widely:

'Following speculation that one of our forthcoming visiting speakers Randy P may pull out amidst safety concerns the University management would like reassure all students, staff and interested parties that the event will go ahead as planned.

We, as an institution, remain committed as ever to an open spirit of debate. We may not always agree but our sites of education must remain spaces where ideas can be heard and be challenged.

We have liaised with Randy P and his staff and have assured them that we will work closely with police to ensure increased security at the event so that it may go ahead in the proper conduct.'

Jane   Dr Hoeffershcheid you are fucking kidding me right?

Hoefferscheid   I'm not going to get drawn on this here Jane.

Jane   Good. I'm blocking you. Fuck you.

Ruth   shit. shit shit shit.

Jane   Shit's about to get real. Here's a link to legal advice when dealing with the police at protests. It contains a list of your rights, of what you do and don't have to tell them, and a legal support number you can call if you get in trouble. Ruth, please share this widely amongst your friends? Make sure the younger people have it. And if you're coming to protest the event tomorrow don't go alone.

Pause.

Ruth   Ok

Loud noise. A short burst of static.

Courtney   Everyone. I don't care about being public about this anymore, the assholes at the student paper have taken over this story since it got big. Please don't read it and support my new free blog site instead. Please boycott the student paper alongside the national news outlets who picked up my words without credit. Click here for my rapid response piece on the clashes between feminist activists, Randy P supporters and riot police happening RIGHT NOW:

RANDY P EVENT MARRED BY WAVE OF PROTESTS

'Student activists protesting the alleged hate speech of alt right figure Randy P were met with riot police on campus today. Police have been attempting to separate the protest from a large and growing faction of free speech activists, MRAs and white nationalists marching through campus. Events are ongoing.'

Follow me for live updates and please like and share. And boycott the student paper. Please.

Hornsby   Look. I can't claim to know what's going on round here these last few weeks since William said that dumbass thing to that young lady. And I don't really think I understand the young folks and their identity politics and their triggering warnings and what-have-you-nots. It would be nice to understand it but I don't. But here's the thing. It's not my job to understand. What I see here are some young folks – good young folks who I know, who pass through my sports teams – who're asking folks to be decent to each other, more or less. And I see some lonely, silly little boys who're more deserving of pity than of scorn trying to push them around for doing so. There's a demonstration of sorts and though I don't know too much about protests and so on and so forth, I think these are principled young ladies and boys, trying to keep on in the world. And I think they need our support.

Barrett   John. John did you hear, I'm keeping my job. They're letting the booby slide – to coin a phrase. The unofficial word is they don't want to be seen as censorious after all this hullaballoo about free speech. So it's a wrap on the knuckles and we move on. Great news right?

Courtney   Anyone? Anyone? Hello? Shit!

Courtney *disappears*.

Barrett   John? John, are you there?

Connor   Hello everyone. Posting this from inside the free speech demonstration. It's getting pretty ugly down here. They've been pushing people around, throwing punches. A woman got punched, on the other side. In the head. There was blood. I think the paramedics came but I couldn't see, they split the groups up and herded us away. There are chants that I won't repeat. It's mostly Randy P supporters and well – they're fascists. They're actual fascists. I want to get out. But the police are herding us together, penning us in. I don't know why I'm posting this here. I came down on my own and I'm scared. I'm really, really scared.

Jane   I thought you were going to defeat them in the marketplace of ideas.

Connor   This isn't the time to take the piss Jane. You sound more like Hannah every day. I take it she's over with your lot, leading the rabble.

Jane   You know what? She stayed at home. She was too scared to leave the house. I read what they sent her, I don't blame her. I guess you can empathise with being scared now too huh? I posted some legal advice perhaps you should take a look. Lesson learned Connor. Red lines.

When you hold open the door for Nazis don't be surprised when they trample over your *nuance*

Connor   I'm blocking you now fuck you.

Connor *disappears. Loud noise. A short burst of static.*

Barrett   'Feminist, LGBT, and anti-racist activists clashed with riot police on an esteemed University campus today after a decision to allow a controversial lecture from visiting speaker Randy P go ahead sparked protests which quickly escalated. Several arrests have been reported including one of the ring-leaders of the protesters, Feminist Society spokesperson Jane Jennings, who had earlier posted the following on Facebook:'

Jane   The only response to fascism is to refuse to countenance it. Our grandparents knew this, we know this. This is what happens. This is what happens when you lay down to Nazis and give a platform to their bullshit. To countenance this ideology is to be complicit in its rise. We will not stand for it.

Jane *disappears.*

Hoefferscheid   'Early reports suggest some staff were among those involved in the fracas, including much-respected community figure Coach John Hornsby, who was photographed amongst the young feminist activists confronting riot police. Mr Hornsby was allegedly seen putting his body between young students and the advancing police lines. His position within the University will now surely be called into question.'

Hornsby *disappears.*

Hoefferscheid   I commend the management on their principled stance. We have always been aware of the strong feelings held about this event but remain unwavering in our commitment to free speech. These are our principles. We will not bend them.

Hoefferscheid *disappears.*

Anna   'Several injuries have been reported in the clashes, with some students being rushed to hospital. Sources can confirm that among that youngest demonstrator hospitalised is first year student Ruth Holybank . . .'

Barrett   ' . . . who had earlier taken to social media to state:'

Ruth   I don't know much about these things. and I know it's complicated. I don't think Connor is a bad guy and I see his point. but I also know what happened when the Nazis won. and I know what I think of what this man says and I know it's wrong. and that's how I know what side I'm on. and that's why I'm joining the protests, and that's why I hope you'll come too.

Jane taught me this new phrase I'd never heard before. I like it because it's clear. it makes a kind of sense to me, cutting through the crap. it's from the Spanish Civil War where they fought the fascists and everything. it means 'they shall not pass.' and it's what I'll be saying if they try to clear us off, to try to let that man speak. to spread his poison.

No pasarán. No pasarán. No pasarán.

Barrett   'Family and friends' posts on Ruth's Facebook page suggest her condition is serious.'

Ruth *disappears.*

Barrett   'A wave of pro-free speech demonstrations in support of Randy P and the University management marched through campus, stopping to protest particularly outside the department of Sociology which houses Gender Studies and the Centre for Postcolonial Studies. Police have sent students and staff from these and other departments in the Humanities away from campus to avoid further conflicts. Groups of young white nationalists were heard chanting about burning books and cheering as buildings were closed and students were sent away by police. Their banner reads: "end political correctness now – we'll say what we want".'

Anna   Slutgate really got out of hand fast, huh? Honestly this place.

Anna *disappears*.

Barrett   Friends, colleagues, family. Just to say I'll be stepping away from Facebook for some time as I take a well-earned research sabbatical to begin writing my new book, on the civil rights movement. It's been a tough few months. Sharing this story here before I go so all of you can understand the menace of the threat to campus free speech from militant young students. I'd like to thank the police for their efforts to maintain order, and thank all of you for your support.

Barrett *disappears*.

Loud noise. A short burst of static.

Preston   this is about a sending a message. to the feminists. the SJWs. the libtards and the thought police. we're pushing back. we're a generation who've taken the red pill, we've opened our eyes and we're not going back in the box you wanna force us in to. sure we're men. sure we're white. but we're not ashamed of it. we're not going anywhere and we're taking back what you took from us. and we're winning. britain has taken their country back. america is being made great again. we're in the driving seat, we're cruising and all you can do is shout from the sidewalk as you eat our dust bitches. you precious little snowflakes can run to your safe spaces all you like. they won't be safe forever

I was there you know. when we shut your places down. gender studies. social studies. all the shit. the strongholds of your politically correct bullshit worldview. we shut them down. and I was there. and the news cameras were there. and the whole world was watching you can't ignore us any longer. you can't ignore me any longer. you all fucking know who I am now. and I'm not going anywhere. so listen up because guess what, snowflakes i hate you all

Loud noise. The sound of static rising in pitch and intensity. It drowns out any other sound, becoming deafening. It cuts out. Silence.

Blackout.